In the Spaces Between Us

In the Spaces Between Us

Poems by

Yvonne Higgins Leach

© 2023 Yvonne Higgins Leach. All rights reserved.
This material may not be reproduced in any form, published,
reprinted, recorded, performed, broadcast,
rewritten or redistributed without
the explicit permission of Yvonne Higgins Leach.
All such actions are strictly prohibited by law.

Cover image by Janice Wall
Author's photo by Ed Turner
Cover design by Shay Culligan

ISBN: 978-1-63980-439-9

Kelsay Books
502 South 1040 East, A-119
American Fork, Utah 84003
Kelsaybooks.com

*For my daughters Shaudee and Cora
with all my love*

Acknowledgments

Thanks to the editors of the following online and print journals in which the following poems previously appeared, sometimes in slightly different versions or with different titles:

Apricity Magazine: "May You Revisit This Memory Often"
Bluestem: "Song of the Willow Tree, Age 10"
Borfski Press: "Morning Passing"
Brief Wilderness: "Walking Shelter Dogs"
Broken Plate: "Iridium"
Brushfire: "On the Origin of My Brother"
Bryant Literary Review: "Absence Doesn't Make the Grass Softer"
Buddhist Poetry Review: "Tides"
Cascadia Rising Review: "My Brother Fishes Lake Curlew"
Caveat Lector: "I Wasn't Looking for a Metaphor"
Clover: A Literary Rag: "Holy Cross Cemetery"
Common Ground Review: "The Authority of Temperatures," "The Clock Key"
Edison Literary Review: "Captive"
Gival Press: "Seven Pounds of Trash a Day"
Glassworks: "Island Tribute to My Lover's Parents"
Hawaii Pacific Review: "Cartoon Character (or Not)"
Hitchlit Review: "Impartial Memories," "Modern Day Blackfoot"
Hobart: "What the Dark Reveals"
Ideate Review: "Seven Pounds of Trash a Day"
Ignation Literary Magazine: "Death Photographer, Mid-1800s," "On My First Imprint of Womanhood"
The Lake: "Upon Glacier Okjukull"
Levee Magazine: "On My Father's Birthday"
Loch Raven Review: "Sunshine Mine Disaster, 1972"
The MacGuffin: "What Is Mine to Claim," "Honoring Meadowbrook"
Neologism Poetry Journal: "Songbird"
Nixes Mate Review: "At Once"
Nude Bruce Review: "25 Items," "Meditation"
Penumbra: "My Best Friend's Mother Paints Her Nails"

Phantasmagoria: "Duty"
Pink Panther Magazine: "Perfect Day," "Among the Pines," "The Practice Of"
Potomac Review: "The Ancients"
Raven Chronicles: "The Belief in Ravens"
RAW: "First Morning in Sedona"
Scriberus Press: "Buzzwinkle"
Silver Birch Press: "The Clock Key"
Spokesman-Review Inlander Magazine Special Edition: "I Wasn't Looking for a Metaphor"
Spotlong Review: "Feeding Time"
The Steam Ticket: "After Snowmelt"
Streetlight Magazine: "Return to My Old Neighborhood"
Streetlight Press: "Middle Seat"
Suisun Valley Review: "First Confession"
Tuck Magazine: "If You Die Alone and Your Body Unclaimed Pray You Die in Pierce County, Washington"
Tule Review: "My Mother's Pajamas"
Voices de la Luna: "Reporting from Their Homes During the Pandemic"
Whitefish Review: "The Volunteer Dog Walker"
Wild Roof Journal: "Unanswered"
Willow Springs Books Zodiac Poetry Series: "Temporary"
Willawaw Journal Poetry & Art: "Moth Snowstorms"

Thank you to the long line of mentors, friends, and fellow poets who helped me shape these poems and this book, especially Alex Kuo, Susan Rich, Susan Lynch, Lea Galanter, Bryn Gribben, Bev Rupp Fesharaki, Elena Olsen, Carrie Simpson, Donna James, Deborah Bacharach, Miriam Bussak, Kathryn Thurber-Smith, Laura Lippman, R. J. Keeler, Linera Lucas, Michelle Bombardier, and Mary Ellen Talley. A deep gratitude to my partner Ed and my siblings. And to my daughters Shaudee and Cora for inspiring me every day to keep creating poems.

Contents

ONE

At Once	17
Among the Pines	18
Perfect Day	19
If You Die Alone and Your Body Unclaimed	
Pray It Happens in Pierce County, Washington	20
Duty	21
My Brother Fishes Lake Curlew	22
Beliefs About Ravens	24
Buzzwinkle	25
Walking Shelter Dogs	26
Upon Glacier Okjukull	27
After Snowmelt	28
Feeding Time	29
Middle Seat	31
Return to My Old Neighborhood	32
Impartial Memories	33
The Authority of Temperatures	34

TWO

Song of the Willow Tree, Age 10	37
First Confession	38
My Name Is	40
Beyond the Senses	42
The Ancients	43
On My First Imprint of Motherhood	44
Morning Passing	46
My Mother's Pajamas	47
The Clock Key	48

25 ITEMS
    We Gather to Divide Our Mother's Possessions   49
Absence Doesn't Soften the Grass   52
I Wasn't Looking for a Metaphor   53
Christmas Tree   54

THREE

Iridium   57
Interruption   59
Reporting from Their Homes in a Pandemic   60
Cartoon Character (or Not)   61
Temporary   62
On the Origin of My Brother   63
Sunshine Mine Disaster, 1972   64
The Death Photographer, Mid 1800s   65
Songbird   66
Modern Day Blackfoot   67
Seven Pounds of Trash a Day   68
Moth Snowstorms   70
Holy Cross Cemetery   72
Meditation   73

FOUR

My Best Friend's Mother Paints Her Nails   77
May You Revisit This Memory Often   78
On My Father's Birthday   79
Honoring Meadowbrook   80
First Morning in Sedona   81

Unanswered	82
Captive	83
The Volunteer Dog Walker	84
Language We Use	86
What the Dark Reveals	88
Island Tribute to My Lover's Parents	89
Tides	90
Visiting My Sister's Island Home	91
What Is Mine to Claim	93
The Practice Of	94
After Wildfires	95

*Love is our true destiny.
We do not find the meaning of life
by ourselves alone—
we find it with another.*
—Thomas Merton

ONE

At Once

North of the peninsula
we can see for miles on both sides:
barns, farmhouses, and how the deep
measure of light
tongues the tall grass.

The North Atlantic wind
beats into our faces.
Sea arches, salt spray, the smell of peat.
Sometimes I wish for better days,
but not today.

You slow the car—
what was vast is now singular.
A tribunal of cows saunters
across the road
from one field to another.

Heads hang like lanterns,
a chorus of hooves,
jabbing of shoulder blades.
This procession of trust knows
no timetable.

Be it the sweet prod
of the farmer's voice
or all of us watching
in silence,
we are home.

Among the Pines

The morning news is resin on our hands.
A hard scrub won't do. So, we make
our big decision for the day—we'll hike
to the Rocks of Sharon, up Iller Creek Ridge.
The sinews of bare branches calcify in frost light.
You ahead, the subtle thumping of your boots
on frozen ground, and I still can't slough off
the refugees, boat upended, their bodies
wave-spewn, their lungs water.
What they see last is blue.
We reach the monoliths that for millennia
remain the same, their massive weight
against the sky, surviving all.
I point you north to gaze
the rocky hills pocked with ponds.
Nothing hems us in up here.
We pull apple slices from our packs
and notice the sweat nagging at our shirts.
I remember we're going to dinner tonight with friends.
What wine should I bring?
For now we sit among the pines.

Perfect Day

for Jono

Under the shade of the wide-leafed Maple,
turning your waffle cone to catch
the rivulets of Rocky Road, you casually
mention that when you were homeless
you played a piano in an abandoned house.

How the light left long shadows, how the temperature
dropped in your skin, how you scrabbled long enough
the house whispered to you, like the fox underneath
the backyard brambles when you were twelve,
before your episodes began and your parents went quiet.

Windows crusted with icy condensation,
walls fended off sleet and anxiety,
the scritch of a skunk perhaps, under
the floorboards, the smell of emptiness.
A Baldwin souring in the corner of the living room.

Days of boredom, yet half-warmth. Nights
dreaming your hands were amputated.
One soft hour, the light broke across the keys and
you played your radiant music so long
and so loud, you stitched notes to the sky.

If You Die Alone and Your Body Unclaimed
Pray It Happens in Pierce County, Washington

Your local government takes over.
Late August, the patrol boat motors out,
the cremated remains of fifty-five
residents stored at the feet of the medical examiner.

The staffer knows it's time to stall,
the haloed head of Mount Rainier towering,
a cerulean horizon perfectly seamed
between water and sky.

All that is known:
name, age, and death date
recited from the hospice chaplain's lips.
Each time, a staffer rings a small bell.

The death investigator recounts
his failures to find family.
Other staffers shake the plastic bags,
ash and knots of bone hit the water

like gravel scattering across pavement.
It's as if, tongueless, they say
one last time
Here I am.

The last cloud of ash-mist floats
in a ragged circle above the boat.
The boat leans away from mended water.
A good day's work.

Duty

The downstairs den glows with late-night TV.
My mother settles into *Doctor Zhivago*
after a day of caring for the six of us.

When I walk in with my lungs on fire
asthma clenches them into rattle and wheeze.
The room is full of air, air stretches through the house

and outside, above other houses
and as far as the moon.
But the right-in-front-of-me air wants

nothing to do with me.
And I see in my mother's expression
both sympathy and disappointment.

When air doesn't cooperate,
she leads me into the small bathroom,
moves the rug so I don't sit on cold tile,

and turns the squeaky knob for Hot all the way
to the right. Steam rises, misting the mirror first,
then clouds take the toilet, and soon

I am drenched in warm fog,
tracing water droplets with my finger
as they run jagged down the wall,

my other hand in my mother's hand.
In time, a strong breath pries open my lungs.
She gives me a squeeze, and then lets go.

My Brother Fishes Lake Curlew

From my cabin porch
    I see him
standing at dock's end

rod in hand
    like an extended appendage
carved-out dawn above

the unruffled water.
    He'll be there all morning
casting and re-casting

conversing with silence.
    How is it that
in hiddenness

he sees a flash
    of silvery scales
sees iridescence

a mouth wide and ready?
    Poised above
the jewel-like scattering

of sun on water,
    he waits
sometimes hours

for the next fish
    to ghost up
from the depths.

He sees water
    the way a fish views it—
egoless, forgetting

worldly desires
    excesses, and discarding
regrets.

I admire his cell
    -like humility
his gratitude for

what is given
    from the water—
its miraculous things.

Beliefs About Ravens

Who conjures up such comparisons?
The souls of evil priests trapped
in their black, oily plumage.
Exorcised spirits croaking
in the deep *crruck-crruck-crruck*
of their call. For the flock
to be called an "unkindness."
Seen as only
antics on a telephone wire,
scrabbling on the sidewalk,
or every task composed of selfishness.

Again this day is rollicking fun
with sticks in their heavy-duty beaks,
beaks that just moments ago
preened one another into a tidy bond.
I hear a chorus and not clatter.
I see cool practice in capturing
every potential kernel.
I encounter play in their
cocking side glances.
Nothing but pure, magnified existence.
I go outside to replant the empty pots.
The ravens remember my face
and trust I mean no harm.

Buzzwinkle

That's what the citizens of the small
Alaskan town name him when he stands

drunk and slightly knock-kneed in the pub's
courtyard after eating too many fermented crabapples.

His inclined head droops under the weight
of his antlers. In shapes of plates and bowls,

they tilt when he turns his long face sideways.
The flap sways under his throat.

All eighteen hundred pounds of him, cinnamon-colored
and sedentary against the dusk,

the hairy shoulder hump, and the huge cupped ears.
Room for wildness here,

from uncultivated land to conversations
unrestrained after having a few

(Heck, even the beasts
get drunk!)

The men feel a safe alliance in his lounging.
Then, a sudden snort through his blunt snout,

as if to say, *I'll take my leave.*
His enormous backside to them now,

his hooves clop on the pavement
in his slow-paced exit toward home.

Walking Shelter Dogs

I tell them the best moments are when
it's just you and the dog out in the field
when the sunlight braids itself in the tall grasses
and the birds gossip and flit in the nearby tree line.
You arrive at the memorialized bench
where the plaque thanks a dead volunteer.
As you both sit there
you run your hand down his back
and rub his chest as he takes a deep breath
and sighs. You say a few kind words to him
and think about your own
abandonment:
when your sister forgot to pick you up from school
when your best friend made out
with the boy she knew you liked
and you weren't friends any more
when the parent you adored
broke open with a terrible imperfection.

Upon Glacier Okjukull

August 2019, Iceland

A hundred people hiked in silence
To the last dangling melt of pure water
To what is now the lost language of ice.
A funeral for a dead glacier, white mass
Turned to dirt and skree under their feet.
Where is the turquoise blue, a child asks.

After Snowmelt

an eloquence emerges:
a birdsong, a feast of wildflowers,
water falling in flight.

The salmon, wolves, beetles,
bull trout, mushrooms, caribou,
the cougars, beavers, and bears

in their broadened wild spaces
astonish the landscape.
And in the sky, too—

a huge cloud drift
changes shape, woven by wind.
Whether air or earth

with no human presence here,
the language of this poem
remains nonviolent.

Feeding Time

Dad gave us permission to save some bread
from the basket. Always a special occasion
when we went to the Italian place at the edge of town.
Always on a Sunday night.

We folded pieces in paper napkins.
Watched the cigarette burn to my mother's fingertips
and when she pressed the red butt hard into the ashtray
and the last of the red wine slipped down her throat

we knew we were on our way,
all six of us, crusts left on checkered tablecloths,
the patrons turning to look
at the child-storm leaving the building.

Did you know the pond still rests there?
The edges rough and mud-ridden.
They can't be, of course, but they look like
the exact same ducks, black beaks and beady eyes.

My brothers rushed ahead, the late light
glazing the sides of tree trunks.
Metallic, sheen heads, incessant quacking
and scurrying done the web-footed way.

My sisters and I held the edge more carefully,
tossed more daintily. What freshness at the sight
of creatures so wild and wanting from us.
Our bellies full; we delighted in feeding them.

I did not want it to end.
The pushing past, the water-pecking,
the necks striking skyward to jolt a piece
down their throats. They'd take a finger off if we let them.

I flicked a piece as if it were a coin, as if to make a wish.
Here's a stroke of luck, I said. I was a stage performer,
a child-goddess, a wild-human creature.
To them, I was all there was. I was legendary.

Middle Seat

In the aluminum tube
with recycled air circulating,
we find our spaces
and shove our possessions
overhead or underfoot.
One of us shoulders the window,
another the open aisle,
and I in the middle seat
graze each of you unintentionally
in my attempt to settle in.

You, young one, to my left
EarPods in, lean your forehead
on the frame and close your eyes.
You, at my right, pull out a thick document
and begin highlighting key sentences.

The thrum of engines,
the horizon flashing by,
the impetus to lift toward sky—
self-propelled and exposed
out toward our destination.
As we slice through the blue air
and over the silver-studded hills,
I will never know whether
you are coming or going,
if you have family you like
and some you don't,
or your take on God,
if you have one.

Even in the moment
of turbulence, we look
straight ahead.

Return to My Old Neighborhood

As I pass the willow-lined pond,
the wheels on my bike click over new cement cracks
from the toll of winter's thaw.
How is it that not much has changed?
The arms of the same cedars droop over the same sidewalks.
Patches of drenched lawn sprout through snow,
and the two-story houses still sit clotted in time.
The early spring sun braids through the pine-dotted park.
I turn the familiar corner toward
my elementary school; the now-faint rain paints
a black scrawl across the playground. The old oak
we climbed, stark gray trunk blotched and bare like a ghost,
welcomes me to come sit again among her branches.
Whenever I return, I ask:
Is it a dying or a new breath?
A robin lands in a nearby vacant lot,
twitches its tail twice
and drops a seed.

Impartial Memories

Not my first time overnight in an airport hotel
in a foreign country. A pre-dawn flight out means
I kill time walking cobblestone streets. The town
in *riposo* so I enter other spaces—

the shadows of shutter-dressed apartments,
garbage cans sunstruck and weighty on curbs,
surprisingly, inside the local cemetery.
Here, photographs adorn above-ground graves.

I leave and think ironically,
Nothing much to do here but live.
I, a passerby, a temporary fixture,
never to return again, will sleep worry-free

in my soundproof room tonight.
When asked about my trip I will go on
and on about the cathedrals, castles, villas, and museums,
the pastas, cheeses, and wines. And yet,

my quiet neighborhood walk amid white stucco,
red roofs, unfamiliar trees, and the sound of the local
church bells ringing, that's a memory I like too—
and the Italian cat on the windowsill closing her eyes to the sun.

The Authority of Temperatures

At the bottom of the hill, I drive left
to see if the grass meadow
has changed color behind the roadside poplars.
The slant of sunlight. The authority of temperatures.
The time of year. Shades move
from yellow to silver to brown
and on this unrepeatable day
to a rich jade. The meadow flashes by
between one poplar and the next.
Often, I spot the horses' heads bent for feeding.
It's a lucky day when I see one lying down
or trotting toward the tree line,
head waving as if pushing air aside,
backside gleaming in the sun or rain.
Today, the day gives me a gift
when the foal appears knock-kneed
next to its mother, neck stretched under her belly
for the lush flow of milk. To think
my dull workdays now start
and end with a mare and her foal.
To think the world so new and open and unbreakable.

TWO

Song of the Willow Tree, Age 10

Up the muscular trunk,
into the artery of the main plank,
and out over the marsh of Cannon Hill pond.
Radiant light sleeps on the silvered tips
of the leaves, still as a whisper.
Settling into a curve, I am
too young to name this pleasure.
So profound is the grass light,
there is even wood light, and the clouds
sing celtic along the edge of sky.

First Confession

Mid-March and we stand
in a fidgety procession,
our whispers echo off
marble walls like moths
against glaring lightbulbs.
We slide onto the wood pews,
shouldering our classmates
into position.
An occasional giggle,
a foot-bang against the kneeler,
and Sister Dorothy furrows
her deep forehead.
Flustered, we thumb the hymnals,
doubting we can unpin
the words from our throats—
words that will declare
our small sins in the dark
air-choked box of the confessional.
Mary Kay Kelly is the first to exit
and all we see is her draping black hair,
pleated plaid skirt and blue knee highs.
How sinful can her seven-year-old life be?
Our hands sweat as we
recite our sins in our heads,
some kind of moral laundry list
      Lied to my mother
      Swore at the neighbor kid
      One day, didn't do my chores.
Spring is upon us
and we're wishing for kickball,
jump rope, hopscotch and fresh air
to swipe our cheeks to red swaths
that stay through fifth period.

The statues of saints in the enclaves
peer down on us and we're wondering
how they lived holier and holier lives.
They do not answer us.

My Name Is

The crucifix on the corner living room wall,
the rosary placed in the dresser drawer,

the family Bible bookmarked on a nearby shelf,
the Irish Catholic name.

The repetition of
Catharines, Margarets, Megans

Theresas and Patricias.
The many combinations of Mary:

Mary Ann, Mary Ellen,
Mary Frances and Mary Grace.

Our name hinged us to our heritage,
echoed off tongues with familiarity,

created alliances with dead relatives.
But with me, all tradition cracked—

what were my parents thinking?—
naming me after my mother's bridesmaid.

She moved far away after the wedding,
maybe even to France.

I was unhinged for ten years, anonymous
among my siblings and cousins,

with no connection
to an aunt, a grandmother, even a saint,

until one day my mother said,
wiping her hands dry on the dish towel,

*Later today, you will meet the woman
you are named after, but for now go outside and play.*

When the car pulled up the gravel drive,
I came from my fort in the woods.

Nervous, I took my mother's arm.
The car door opened and out stepped a woman

into the warm summer air named Yvonne.

Beyond the Senses

How the light leads me down
two flights of stairs, my feet avoid
the creaks, my frame small against
the biceps of furniture. How,
because it is spring, I need only
a light jacket and slip-on shoes.

In the meadow, the wash of
dewy grass wets my shoes.
How when the birds summon
the morning, I am unafraid,
and nothing but clear air
sops up the sky.

How upon entering the forest,
the trunks are wild and perfect,
and the scent of ponderosa pine blossoms.
I tip my head to the canopy,
specks of blue breaking through,
and something comes beyond the senses,
beyond the edge of the world,
catches my breath and calls me.
Without effort, I am more than I am.

I run back home and shake my parents awake
announcing something outside came to me,
and because I cannot name it
they turn over under the covers and tell me
to go back outside and play.

The Ancients

I refuse to read the plaque at the trailhead
on the disappearance of big-treed forests.
Refuse to read of industrial scale,
mechanized clear-cutting to feed a ravenous
global market. How only ten percent
of the forests of giants remain. How what
was lush, thick and dense is now stagnant air.

Instead, I choose to walk among them
and ponder:

How it goes with the ancients,
fringed with lichen, their bark
flakes and sheds—a look gained
from great age. They soar up
through the centuries, canopies
in tiers of decades gone by. Where ancients
have fallen, sunlight pours down in gaps
and young ones surge skyward.

Below, the soil is dark like ink,
rich like chocolate. Fungi is alive
in the dank underbelly of logs and nooks
and crooks, in the gothic-shaded network
of roots, snags, branches and ferns.

So much becomes nests for birds and dens for bears.
Weathermakers, food creators, holders of
molds and slimes and moss. What is most amazing
I don't know—how what takes centuries to grow
takes longer to die, yet still nurtures life.

On My First Imprint of Motherhood

Because my mind is a bank
of images sparked by emotion

I see you come through the door, Auntie,
in your wrinkled receptionist uniform

the last half mile of dirt road you took
spit up dust in makeshift shapes that

touch down as altars of anxiety
when the sun gushes into the empty

space where his truck should be.
Your heart abandoned as he fists

a cold beer at the bar.
The repeat cycle of

Will he come home tonight, or not
engraved like map lines on your pale face.

Only fifteen, I kill a perfectly good
summer day, watch daytime soaps

and read *Seventeen* magazine
from the indent in the couch.

I half-watch my rugrat cousins pounce
from rock to rock in the river all morning

then barrel in for a bowl of cereal
and run back out again, barefoot with the sun.

You pull a pan from the cupboard
and complain of a headache.

I set the table and when you hand me his favorite mug
a lightning storm of *not-me-ever* courses in my heart.

When night fell it was always the same:
you dream of the wonderful man you never met.

The next morning you made enough
coffee to fill his thermos.

Morning Passing

They both passed in their back bedroom,
in the same type of brought-in hospital bed,
three years and two months apart.
Dad first. Then Mom.

Both in morning. The start of birds' waking,
whirling, chirping, the notes singing up
and down their throats, an orchestra
claiming another day of living.

My Mother's Pajamas

I took one pair not thinking
they would fit, but they did.
Cotton, green with thin, white and purple stripes,
pull-string bottoms,
they still carry your smell of Nina Ricci.
I wear them on hard days
when missing you hits me
like hard weather,
and on easier days too when
I think I can be strong again.
I wash them by hand so as
not to wear them out because
what will I do then?

The Clock Key

First it was Dad. Then Mom
passed. We divided up their possessions
diplomatically among the five of us.
Among them, two antique, wind-up wall clocks,
and a nine-foot-tall Hamilton Grandfather from Pennsylvania.
Years later, my sister finds
a small brass key
in a tattered, two-inch, yellow envelope
in my mother's jewelry box.
In cursive, my mother wrote: Clock Key.
So my sister makes the rounds with it,
an excuse for a visit,
but none of us want to try it
because we like that, somehow,
our clocks keep ticking ahead, regardless.

25 ITEMS
We Gather to Divide Our Mother's Possessions

    i.   Firstborn Daughter

This poem should start with us entering the apartment
in morning light, but before that we needed a process

because I am a lawyer and like logic,
how one step occurs before another toward a goal.

I also am the executor of the will
and take my responsibility seriously.

The coffee table laden with lamps. Vases bulge
on the mantel. Dishes dress the kitchen counter.

Room to room, as if in a museum, we get an hour
to pick the top five items that mean most to us.

    ii.   Oldest Son

A frost-covered February morning
    the apartment exactly   as Mom had left it.

I open the blinds   like she would have.
Her caretaker from afternoon

to bedtime for years, I know how the light
    invites shadows   on the walls,

the creaky complaint   of the bathroom door,
how to fold and stack the linen towels.

I love how a poem is written in sections
    like this one   like these objects in their spaces.

iii. Middle Son

Like most of my life, I arrive
on time. Listen. Follow the instructions.

The smell of coffee lingers.
Languid light nudges us along.

Pen and paper in hand,
I write a list poem today.

An owl statue, a hand-painted bowl,
coasters, and books about Montana.

How I wish I had asked more
about her life.

iv. Second Daughter

Happy to support my sister
               in creating the process

but today is about the wood-carved sculpture
               of mother and child adorning the dresser.

And the story that goes with it.
               God, how I adore symbolism.

A life's division
               is not left in lightless basement boxes.

We carry them to our homes—
               each has a voice and sings!

v. Youngest Son

We name the heirlooms we picked and say why.
Amazingly, no duplicates, no tussles, no conflict.

Maureen picked the everyday dishes,
shared memories of special meals.

Tim picked a set of books on Montana,
said he loved them since he was a boy.

Like the perfect rhythm of a poem,
each commentary flowed.

Through objects, anecdotes about our mother
are alive in the modest afternoon light.

Absence Doesn't Soften the Grass

Seeing that my dog is old and dying, my neighbor said:
That's why I never got one. Truth is, they always die before you do.

And so I walked Gus over to him, close enough for his furry head
to meet his calloused hands. With a wet-nose nudge, Gus looked
    up
in an act of faith, and the dead bird inside my neighbor's heart
    broke open.

I Wasn't Looking for a Metaphor

I was looking for the right wave
to wash the sand from my hands.

So many waves laddering across the shoreline
in predictable time, yet my hands remained rough.

And I thought of you,
in the lip of the front porch frame,

your silhouette distinct in the lucid light,
your arms full of things whose smells

made no sense to me—
homemade brownies and fresh flowers.

When you whispered, *I hope it is okay to just drop by,*
I felt an exhaustion buck my ribs, reminding me

that for several weeks now I hadn't talked
about my loss. That day, only safe, unhurtable words.

You stepped in, humbly
placed your gifts on the entry table

and kept the air just the right
space between us.

Christmas Tree

inspired by poet Connie Wanek

To stand tall but not in earth
to survive in plastic and faucet water
to live for wearing colored lights
to ignore the four walls and no sky
to show off ornaments and still be simple
to be evergreen and oxygen and holiday spirit
to bless the one family who picked you.

THREE

Iridium

for Bill

He rolled the silvery-
    white element from his palm up
        to his fingers and back again.

You asked: *What is that*
    you hold in your hand?
        And he spoke

of all things iridium—
    the rarest metal
        in the world, more valuable

than gold.
    So sell this when I'm gone,
        he winked.

And there was more—
    It's used in spark plugs
    and compass bearings.

Compass bearings, you think.
    You like that, knowing how
        he helped you find your way

again, and taught you about the maze
    of pathways in the mind,
        and the mystery of star clusters.

How can so much hinge on
    something this hard and brittle?
        A small, square piece

of metal that for years
   held down one paper pile
      after another—

became his provider of comfort,
   a touchstone for his good ideas.
      You sold it after his death

and never doubted once.
   You knew it was love
      the whole time.

Interruption

It's the skirt hitting a woman's face
and her polka dot underwear
blinking like a neon sign.
A hat trundling down the street.
An umbrella snapping inside out.
It's the ripples rising on the lake
and rowing frantically to outpace them.
The bird suddenly flying sideways.
The bleating sheep so nervous that his fleece flails.
It's wind's gift of surprises—
these chance encounters with *stop-what-you-are-doing*.
It's not a devasting diagnosis
or a family member dying.
It's a nudge to put aside distractions,
slow our frantic pace of buying groceries and getting gas,
and for us to stop protecting ourselves. And do it right now,
wind or no wind—celebrate the hawk flying overhead.

Reporting from Their Homes in a Pandemic

Rumors all winter and then it felt so sudden;
they had no choice but to let us in. Given the circumstances,
we became their guests. We'd bring a bottle of wine
if we could. They decide the backdrop:
a table vase with pussy willows next to a round mirror.
A painting of forsythia, yellow as goldfinches, wait, or
are those goldfinches? And all those books!
I like to think of his hand pulling down
the biography of Lincoln and handing it to me.
It felt so sudden and now we're tongue-thick
in new phrases: *social distance, safer at home,
flatten the curve.* Under inelegant lights,
a reporter speaks of refrigerator trucks
devastating the side streets of New York City,
and instead, I fancy starting a conversation
about how often she references her copy of
Elements of Style. Another night, I buzz
from the reporter's repeat messages about
the surge in deaths. All a faint echo as I am distracted
by his columns of rose-colored wallpaper
and a barometer next to his bookshelf.
I'd like to think, my glass of wine in hand,
we'd laugh at the irony of the secondary meaning
of barometer. It felt so sudden
and now I find myself exploring
their family photos, framed awards, shapes
of anchored lampshades. I spill into
their living rooms, chipping away their personal anonymity.
Hours between morning and night, our homes
are our safeguards as the world flails.
I wish it all didn't feel so sudden, like when
the season shifts and you fasten your coat.
Books behind your head,
titles sideways on their spines,
I should be listening to what you are saying.

Cartoon Character (or Not)

No man ever told her she couldn't do it herself.
Nor did the female cartoon characters who
gleamed on the screen. Even Olive Oyl ate spinach.
With the same superhuman strength, she beat
every boy in the 100-yard dash in the 7th grade.
She never questioned in high school the potential
of her mind. AP Chem. AP Physics.
AP Math. She was Velma leading Scooby Doo
and the gang to the crook behind the mask.
Finding independence in college, she explored
sexuality, politics, and religion. Like Wonder Woman
she reconciled the various competing parts of herself.

***

It's fifteen years later and the plot twist is:
she and her husband pull weeds
in the backyard as their 6-year-old
throws a ball. When he runs to get it
the husband yells: *Don't run like a girl!*
She feels her insides whip up a force field,
and the warrior power of the Avatar universe
pulses through her body. She stands up
as Suki and kicks her husband's ass.

Temporary

The dogs' yelps smash chaos
against the cement walls, metal cages,
florescent lights.

The volunteer leads me
to the back right corner
where the little black lab mix

with a temporary name
is a dark lump trembling
near her spilled water dish.

> "Chained in yard, all day, every day, in all conditions."
> I see the box marked *Neglected*
> and try not to think of cold rain,

soggy fur, whimpering.
Shitting and pissing in one small circle.
Grief-bound in some bare place.

I kneel as if commanded
to be level with her eyes, wishing
I could tell her, *Not everyone is cruel.*

Though my voice
sounds like chimes, I could be winter
or fire to her.

Yet, she inches forward
as if on a thinly frozen pond
and when in reach

she sweetly licks
my fingers through the holes,
tastes my salt.

On the Origin of My Brother

for Tim

In the collision of sperm and egg,
a Creator said, *Let him become.*
A bright mind, a storyteller,
a lover of language,
my brother is an ecosystem
of contrasts. The pleasantries
of life—an evening with family,
a job well done, and the good storm
of children—clash with
the cement forests of too much drink,
the oil spills of overeating,
and the wildfires of gambling.
He lives in a genetic landscape
of addictions.
A life spent wanting
another life.
When finally the seasons added up
and the mountain breathed,
he found a way beyond
the dark and tired nights, beyond
being the helpless animal
forced from home.
He planted a garden
inside himself.
He lives.

Sunshine Mine Disaster, 1972

Kellogg, Idaho

A mine blows up in Idaho near my hometown.
Thirteen men surveyed the unplotted
rock edges in blackness, prayed for days
for a spillage of light down their shaft
and when it didn't come, they murmured
to save every last bit of air, pushed
their prayers from their mouths
to their minds. One miner,
weak and lament-bound,
his hands stretching into
more darkness found a headlamp.
Guys! he shouted, *Look!*
The artificial square of light
flickered and then dimmed.
Just enough light for them to watch
as another miner reached into
his back pocket and unfolded
an insurance form.
Doesn't look like I'll be needing
this any time soon, he laughed.
What they'd give to have to pay a bill.
Amid the dust and hunger, and the sunken
doubt of rescue, they wrote
their goodbyes on the back.
In one miner's strained handwriting:
What I'd do to see
the sky full of white clouds again.

The Death Photographer, Mid 1800s

Mostly children.
He knows composition and light
and exposure. But his honed skill
was in the pose—the baby in peaceful
slumber, the doll placed under the arm
of a young girl, the boy's feet crossed at the ankle.
The mother styling her daughter's hair,
puffing up her dress sleeves
by blowing breath at the cuff.
Their shadows pressed on a plate in precise permanence.
He did what they asked.
Some wanted to add color to the cheeks.
The father who needed help
propping his five-year-old son against a wooden box.
Dressed and suddenly standing in his cotton shirt,
knickers and boots. He didn't say no when
the mother asked if it was *too much* if she put
a bouquet of wildflowers from her garden in his hand.
Beyond the flowers were the boy's eyes.
And when they couldn't do it, he stepped around
his camera and opened them,
the reflecting light made him question the boy's dead heart.
Perfect, they say, this is exactly
how we want to remember him.

Songbird

Once a week
                mail in hand
       oxygen tank dragging
she enjoys
                the pleasure of fresh air.

She wears a clean house dress
                and while the wheels
       over the sidewalk
go cu-clunk, cu-clunk
                she feels the cloudy light

as the cooler-than-expected air
                restricts her lungs.
       Her neighbor doesn't
look up
                from watering his patio plants.

She's learned not to care.
                Instead
       when she hears the
elaborate song
                of the Pacific wren

the tune plays
                in her chest, too
       the inhale and exhale
effortless as if
                she were a child again.

She tugs the tank
                around her ankles
       taking the turn
toward home, owning her
                alliance to air.

Modern Day Blackfoot

He is fused to the sun and air
like the wash of light on river water.
His Blood Reservation is a mouth
that speaks of tree-blanketed hills
prairieland, badger, elk
berry, bear and wolf.
He speaks to wolves.
After a date with his wife
he drives her in his slick-black Chevy Silverado
large hands at the wheel
headlights breaking through
the drench of darkness
up the meandering road
and into the pullout
across from the burned-out aspen stand.
They step out
under the star-magnified sky
engine off but clicking
like an irritated insect.
Belly River bulges
from the springtime snowmelt.
The Belly River wolf pack
in the windless night
rest near their den
accustomed to the cool earth beneath them.
When he cups his hands and howls
down the canyon
they stand up
stretch their throats skyward
and howl back.

Seven Pounds of Trash a Day

and that includes me
and every other American.
Every Thursday on our block
we haul our rotting food scraps,
our #5 and #6 plastic
and Styrofoam containers
to the curb
and I am thinking how
my plastic coffee lid
from Starbucks
will take 20–30 years
to decompose in some
shapeless 300-foot-high
immortal slum of our bygones,
how skittering birds
will drum up
some dead thing
amid the bursting pile
of tormented colors.
Everything inside me
is rattling
like wind driving
at a loose door
for how pithy my
small changes—
not buying plastic
water bottles,
shortening my hot showers,
turning down the heat,
when I too
am part of humanity
that is simply changing
too late,

as if the earth can keep
sustaining us,
as if it's not really
the earth at all.

Moth Snowstorms

Uncle Gordon and Aunt Mary waving
in our rearview mirror. Dad now hours
behind the wheel. Mom up front

while my brother and I share leg space
in the back. We shut our books, surrender
to the twilight-magnified sky, the muggy summer air.

When the curve of earth vanishes
and the nightfall ceilings us, predictably
they arrive—the scale-winged insects

drawn to light like humans to love.
A *bump, bump* against the beam
of headlights. Then *splat, splat*

against the barrier of windshield,
and as if a sudden storm,
the moths are like snowflakes in a blizzard.

White and gray gauzy wings spiral
from their thumb-sized bodies.
They churn in the air as our speeding car

splices the darkness with a harsh
wash of manmade light. An unforgiving hurling.
An assault.

What is now a mural of moths,
likely thousands, like protons,
lurch and throttle until a mash

shuts out the light. My father
slows to the side of the road.
A rag ready under the seat, he steps out

to clean glass surfaces, crusted
with broken limbs, mouthparts, and underwings.
With each forceful swipe, the lights

break brighter, shining on the moth-cluttered
distance behind him, haunting the night.
They're wretches akin to rust, my mother says.

They'll eat your clothes, even your books.
And, all at once, I am startled by my sadness,
at their price of existence,

drawn to what extinguishes them.

Holy Cross Cemetery

after poet and essayist Thomas Lynch

Section G,
just past the tender,

standalone pine,
my parents' stones

next to my sister's
stone, and more stones,

sepulchers and crosses
amid the green hills.

The dead are everywhere,
here for us to remember

them, and I do.
I stand among the stones.

Sometimes I laugh,
sometimes I weep.

Sometimes nothing
much happens at all,

because even in the dull quiet,
in the lack of body-

and-skin smell among
the disappearing light,

this moment
I live in is mine.

Meditation

Elements from inside the furnace
of long-dead stars, new molecules
in the cell walls of bacteria,
atoms from the lungs of my ancestors:
I was formed.
Fused to this world too at the holiest cell level
are the bodies of strangers,
sun-drenched and rainfed like mine.
Beloved, I say:
You are part of me that
I do not know yet.
Braided to each other
like radiant light between leaves,
I say let us abandon religion
for the natural world astonishes.
Let us go back to where we started,
to the grandeur of being a child.
How we pondered the sinewed shape
of the beetle's black back, how we
poked, prodded, studied, and then let it go.
If we hold close this wonder,
that all is made of the stuff of stars,
we will remember how to love again.

FOUR

My Best Friend's Mother Paints Her Nails

Uninvited, I interrupt her
rare moment of quiet.
Her long narrow body dints
the lounge chair cushion
under the porch canopy.
Hard to believe I am alone with her.
No other children darting around
or another meal to make.
A lovely creamy red, her toes dry
in the wash of lucid summer air.
I have known her all my life,
and my adoration grows
as I become my pre-teen body.
I know nothing of where she came from.
Refined, she slides the file
into her leather manicure set.
With shoulder blades like tiny bird bones
above her blouse, she blows softly
her deep-red fingernails.
Swells with the scent of
her perfume waft my way.
Instead of sending me home,
she drenches me in the generosity
of conversation,
pulls my hands close,
and asks me to pick a color.

May You Revisit This Memory Often

Your grandfather's legs your foundation,
forget the white plastic chair holding you both.

Poolside, tops of palm trees seize the breeze
and fronds fill your eyes in a protective dance.

Your legs meld into his, even with the beach towel
damp between you. Your back

leans into his breathing chest, breath
that does not need to form words when

given over to love long ago, at your birth,
the world became yours.

All is confirmed again when you both catch
the red flash of the flycatcher's underbelly.

Your grandfather's large hand in view
and he whispers: *Look!*

On My Father's Birthday

How it is that certain
memories are echoes
loud and repetitive like hearing
a good verb for the first time.

Our birthdays two days apart.
Our breaths meld over
the liquidy light of candles
in a dreamhaze of wishes.

Years now I blow out
candles alone
and the moment the smoke
shapeshifts into invisibility

you come again in another form
rare as the shrill of air passing
through a condor's wings
and I too know the sound of sky.

Honoring Meadowbrook

for Cora

Up against the wetland forest
where bands of light fuse with frosty grass,
the bull's crown of points cuts the sky
like a lapidary cuts stone.
My daughter, new to this small town,
has found the meadow where the elk herd thrives.
This birthplace of the Snoqualmie Tribe.
This *Hyas Kloshe Ilahee,*
their "great good land."
Close enough, we see the bull's exhalation spill
into visible air, others lay their bodies
of thick smooth fur into the earth,
and some graze to fatten up
for the harsh winter ahead.
No haunting bugle, no ritualized rut,
just benevolent existence—
this first witnessing together
of what is holy.
What cannot last
is still a blessing.
The minute we drive away
we make room for this
new song in our hearts.

First Morning in Sedona

Spillage of the mourning dove's lament,
the first-blossom of the spine-birthed cacti,
the stretch of the white-shocked sycamore,
and the sun-crested helmets of red rocks
while scrub oaks thirst in the distance.

We are bound by dust, dry air and this slow hour.

The full-bellied quail bursts from the underbrush,
leans into his curved topknot as if
pushing into wind, and as I hand you tea
the desert bows to your grief,
gives us permission not to speak.

Unanswered

I set down my book in the shadow of the disheveled night,
the never-knowing unraveled. I will never be ten again,
innocently showing off my rabbit's foot keychain.
Engraved in the pages is my never-going-back.
I cannot unsee the minks being pressure-washed
while in their tiny cages,
or the pregnant sow that cannot turn around in her crate,
or the dolphin deprived of food until he learns
to bounce a ball on his nose. The hollow-eyed moon
sweeps my bookshelf, disappointed at how we mis-
understand use and pleasure for our own good.
The world's indecency drowns in suede shoes,
dissections, and zoos.
The ruckus in my mind sees only
straps, traps, snares, whips, guns, drills, cages, and poison.
The cost of loss happens away from my eyes
and it's easy not to ask: At what cost are my bones raised,
and still I do not change my ways?

Captive

Old hotel. Paint peeling, stagnant pool, but a monkey?
Cement floor, rusted cage, no perch. I see movement: sad monkey.

I write the local shelter which says: *report it to police.*
I wake up at night thinking incessantly of the poor monkey.

I research the internet, learn they need to swing, want a high perch.
I decide to report the neglect for the sake of the monkey.

I don't speak the language of this country nor do I know its norms,
but suddenly I find myself impersonating the monkey.

I wonder what they think of me, the white-visored American.
I want to say in Spanish: *he hangs desperately there, the monkey.*

Sound sleep. Days of sun. Good books. Wine under diamond stars.
I ask more questions, becoming more obsessed with the monkey.

Will the police call the hotel? Will they stress enough urgency?
I email again: *Please improve the life of your monkey!*

I thought about dropping by the hotel before leaving but
I doubt they would have made changes so quickly for the monkey?

Instead, I sent something like a love letter off the airplane's wings
as I looked down over the bay where the dear monkey sat.

Comfortably, I hoped, and on a high perch. Even a fast storm
knocking out the city lights can't drape darkness over the monkey.

My vacation over—*how was it?*—everyone always asks.
Good weather, good food, I say, *except that I saw this monkey . . .*

The Volunteer Dog Walker

The Pit Bull Terrier catches my eye.
I stop at his cage and he lunges
from wall to wall, leaps five feet in front of me.

Frenzied, spinning, he knows I mean
sun, fresh air, the earth underfoot.
I go inside and, after several tries, leash him.

He pulls hard in the aisle,
so hard his nails scrape sideways
on the cement floor. My shoulder yanks.

Other dogs anxiously
bark *Walk me, walk me!*
in the purgatory of florescent lights.

We break through the door to the morning light
and air, both widened by the meadows
that surprise. In the play yard, I let him free.

He lumbers, sniffs, then runs the fence line.
At once, he takes a big, steamy shit in the dirt
the way it's supposed to be done.

He was born with the stars against him,
unwanted now more than a year.
Grim are his scraps of days,

the pitiful repetition of basic needs.
He knows nothing of survival
but to do it. After lapping fresh water,

his pink tongue hangs sideways.
Out of breath,
all sixty pounds of him collapse

next to me as I sit on the grass in the shade.
He suddenly can't be hurried,
eyes the horizon beyond the fence.

How is it I behold him as an angel?
Yet I am not his God.
Our doctrine is this quiet moment.

This crack of light in the darkness.
Domesticated bundle of beast before me:
Let's sit together a little while longer.

Language We Use

inspired by Rick Bass

We shrug off language
    to mere fragments,
manipulate it like a rope
    that holds only our agenda.

We settle for it in the medical
    world, the political world,
the world that advantages a company—
    even in how we speak of

the natural world. We
    "eco-manage" our unprotected wild
lands. We become bewildered
    by the "amenities" of grizzly bears

and forests. Our anemic language
    tries to accuse someone, somewhere,
for the disappearing polar-white glacier
    slipping slowly above the ground

as it whispers into vapor, into air.
    We lack words that describe
the permanence of a species extinction,
    we're left to pointing a finger at a photograph.

We even misrepresent what Nature
    does naturally—"insect *epidemics*,"
"*catastrophic* fires"—is it a shield
    we use to bid us a head nod

so we can keep our conveniences?
    Why not words like grace, order

and logic? Why not look at the landscape
    and its species with an electrifying

radiance, a throb of vulnerability of what
    we are in it, not over it—
then might we see ourselves
    for one brief moment

in the shine, the bend, the returning.

The line describing the glacier comes from Ed Roberson's poem "To See the Earth Before the End of the World."

What the Dark Reveals

I wake to the shuffle of wind along the sill.
The soft moon hue weighs on my blanket, saying nothing.
From the fragile dark, experiences remembered
become rocks tied to my ankles and feelings churn for hours.
How in those days I thought I knew myself well, and wonder now
why she seems like a stranger. How in those days I had alliances.
We shared wine and meals, swam in lakes, protested together.
Where are those friends now? Many nights what I wish
would fade away like far-off animal sounds in the hills
edges upward as if I know they are coming
before they are coming. And my mind is on fire.
I wake exhausted, ask if this is my new existence—
this ancestry of flailing memories and broken sleep.
I say no more sloughing off what the dark reveals.
I face the mirror, holding myself and all my shadows.
At first light, I search for photographs,
boxes of letters, report cards, our family tree.

Island Tribute to My Lover's Parents

You come to me in pieces: in the stories your son, my lover,
recalls, in black-and-white photographs

in the desk drawer that I try to imprint on my mind
like tattoos, in the wood-making tools your hands last touched,

in the surprise when I pull a hand-painted English vase
from the back of the kitchen cupboard.

I have come here now, season over season,
here, to this house you both envisioned and built and lived in

for forty-two years. I am the body you once were,
as the salt water latches to my lips,

as the invisible obedience of the moon unveils beach
and rock and kelp, as the ferry to Southworth by day

still gleams white as a horse, by night glows
like a lit birthday cake. From this living room where cancer took

your last breath, the view remains magnificent.
We live with the continuing rhythm, the landscape, the praise of
    song.

Tides

At bedtime, the enormous
labor of buoyancy forces itself against our bulkhead.
By morning, it reverses
and sunlight plays on the sand,
drying the bodies of mud shrimp
that know when
to burrow
based on this timekeeper's waxing and waning.
The tides live in the crabs
in the deepest ocean and the smallest
whirlpools and eddies.
From tide pool to the stars and back again, we witness
daily the paradox
of change and changelessness, every shift a baptism of shore
and the merciful bracing of anemone on rock.
All this cascading
is performed by the resonant call of moon and tides.
Startled when its
white-breasted chest burns through the tree branches,
we are reminded
of this goddess gravity, her invisible vibration,
her obligation
to reveal worlds and then cover them up again.
In her phases of quartering,
she gives us sure-fire tides and that is why I know
on my morning walk
the carpet of shore is shortened by last night's hour.
Yet the jellyfish
with a center the color of eggplant surprises,
waits assuredly in a slant of water.

Visiting My Sister's Island Home

I left behind the basalt rocks
of the scablands

to stand in the fold of
the ocean's pull.

The sand soft under my feet
as the tide

releases her swell.
The robin replaced by

a blinking heron,
her tucked wings lustrous

as her long legs sidestep
the weedy rocks.

Waterlight traces the edge
of shore in white waves.

Like the call of my first-born breath,
I draw salt into my lungs

and as the tilt of light
blends itself mysteriously,

I lift my arms.
There is no in front of me

or behind me.
Unveiled, I am

all air, and no air,
at once.

Call it what you want.
When a bird calls overhead

the way it exists
without thinking of existence

that is me
nowhere but here.

What Is Mine to Claim

I am from a turn-of-the-century home,
from radiators and a laundry chute.
I am from the oak tree in the backyard.
I am from dogs and cats and hamsters,
crucifixes on bedroom walls
and rosaries in our pockets.
I am from lemon pepper chicken, from boxed
yellow cake with chocolate frosting.

I am from lake water, calm or stormy.
Year over year, from jack-o'-lanterns'
faces carved alive, and Christmas trees
lighting the living room corner.
I am from conversations about politics
and religion, from justice-driven relatives,
the Irish famine still deep in their souls.
I'm from O'Driscolls, O'Geraghtys, and O'Higgins clans,
from potatoes cooked every which way.

From the sister who died at 24
in a car accident, from parents who
placed the board across the creek so we could cross.
When I drive through the old neighborhood
past my house, my schools, the parks
and St. Augustine's Church tethered to the hilltop,
somehow the passage of time is okay,
knowing I am from such a place,
such a people.

The Practice Of

A seagull tugs at seaweed.
His thick justice of beak
knows nothing of reluctance.

Something of air, sand and salt
and you are not hanging on
to anything but adoration.

You let go of antics.
You let go of control.

This turmeric sky is
exceptional. You listen and escape
to a breath far lovelier than your own.

After Wildfires

That moment when my daughter has a woman's body,
when my mother can't open a pickle jar,
when my brother moves from manic to calm.

Over seasons, and often quietly,
when I'm not paying attention,
suddenly I am left widened by time.

When that thorn of a bad decision
disappears, and from purgatory I rise
into soft powdery light.

I cannot remember the molting—
that awkward, clumsy uncertainty.
I wake with new pinfeathers.

Let the faithful beast of change
keep breathing. It's after wildfires
when the flowers come.

About the Author

Yvonne Higgins Leach is the author of *Another Autumn* (Cherry Grove Collections, 2014). Her poems have been published in *The South Carolina Review, South Dakota Review, Spoon River Review, The Cimarron Review, POEM,* and others. She spent decades balancing a career in communications and public relations, raising a family, and pursuing her love of writing poetry. Her latest passion is working with shelter dogs. She splits her time living on Vashon Island and in Spokane, Washington.

For more information, visit:
www.yvonnehigginsleach.com

www.ingramcontent.com/pod-product-compliance
Lightning Source LLC
Chambersburg PA
CBHW031200160426
43193CB00008B/455